AF255600

A, B, C, D, E, F, G
Africa
Is Where We'll Be

Authored by Debra Rilley

Illustrated by Patrick L. Hill

Copyright ©2026 Debra Rilley All Rights Reserved
A, B, C, D, E, F, G Africa Is Where We'll Be

ISBN: 978-1-965761-88-5

Library of Congress Control Number: 2026906018

No part of this book may be reproduced, stored in a retrieval system, or transmitted in any form or by any means—electronic, mechanical, photocopying, recording, or otherwise—without prior written permission of the publisher, except for brief quotations in reviews.

Author: Debra Rilley
Illustrator: Patrick L. Hill
Layout Designer: Marigold2k
Publisher: Menagerie Publications
Assisting Publisher: Spotlight Publishing House

Dedication

I dedicate this book to all the children in my life
– past, present, and future –
whose curiosity and spirit have continually inspired me to follow my heart and be my best.
You've reminded me to always strive for excellence, and remain curious.
It is my wish that you will always to do the same!

Preface

Animals live all over our amazing planet.
From icy lands to steamy jungles, wide deserts to deep oceans.
You may already know some of their names,
but there is always more to discover about who they are and how they live.

For every animal in this book, you'll find three adjectives to describe them.
These words will give you new ways to talk, think, and wonder!
I wrote this book for curious readers, big and small, who love animals and enjoy learning.
If you discover a favorite animal or a treasured word along the way,
then this book has done exactly what I intended it to do!

Enjoy reading, and let the journey begin!

Adorable, Attractive, Astonishing African Penguins are among the smallest penguins, reaching only 18 inches tall. They thrive in the heat of South Africa. Believe it or not, they burrow into underground nests to escape the heat and predators! These little penguins have a loud donkey-like call they use to communicate.

Beautiful, Beguiling, Bodacious Beisa Oryx are unmistakable with their straight horns and stunning facial markings. Their nickname is the "spear antelope." This majestic animal thrives in harsh conditions across Eastern Africa. They are one of four species of medium-sized antelope.

Charismatic, Clever, Courageous Cheetahs are the fastest land animal and can run 50-80 miles per hour. Their claws don't fully retract, which gives them an excellent grip for running at high speeds. Cheetah spots are as unique as human fingerprints. They hunt and are active during the day, unlike other big cats!

Diving, Determined, Decisive Duiker Antelope are small, shy animals found in the thick brush and forests all over Africa. They're only 20 inches tall! This delicate antelope takes off at high speeds in a series of diving jumps when alarmed. They can escape predators by swimming away.

Easygoing, Eager, Elusive African Elephants are one of the only mammals that can't jump, and they do not like bees! Their trunks have over 40,000 muscles that are used for smelling, drinking, bathing, lifting, pushing, and manipulating objects. Elephants spend most of their day looking for and eating 100 pounds of food. They are the largest land animals on earth!

Flamboyant, Flirtatious, Frolicking Flamingos are found in shallow wetlands and coastal areas across parts of Africa. They use their beaks and feet to stir up mud and filter out algae, invertebrates, and seeds. When their leg bends, it's the ankle that we see hinging. Their knees are farther up their legs, hidden by their body and feathers!

Grand, Gregarious, Genial Giraffes are the tallest animals on earth. Despite their long necks, they have the same number of vertebrae as humans! Giraffes are herbivores, so they spend many hours a day eating the leaves and twigs of acacia, mimosa, and wild apricot trees. Much like cows, they regurgitate food and chew it again as cud.

Humongous, Harmonious, Happy-go-lucky Hippos spend much of their time submerged in rivers and wetlands. This helps them stay cool and avoid the sun. Their nostrils, eyes, and ears are positioned on the top of their heads, which allows them to breathe, see, and hear while in the water. Hippos feed on vegetation at night and occasionally eat a little fruit!

Impeccable, Impressive, Imperturbable Impalas have tufts of black hair that cover a scent gland just above the heel on each hind leg. When surprised, an impala will leap about, allowing it to release signals from the fetlock scent gland in midair. This keeps the herd together because of this anti-predator technique! Impalas are herbivores and are found in regions with access to water, which is essential for drinking and staying cool.

Jubilant, Jesting, Jiggish Jackals have remained unchanged for over two million years! This was established to be true based on fossil evidence. Jackals are opportunistic omnivores, predators of smaller animals, and proficient scavengers. They howl at night to establish territories, warn of danger, and reunite with their mate.

Kinetic, Kicky, Kittenish Klipspringers are small antelope with hooves that have rubbery centers and hard rims. These hooves provide an excellent grip on steep, rocky terrain. Klipspringers mate for life and are almost inseparable! They take turns watching for danger and ensuring each other's safety.

Laudable, Lithely, Large-Hearted Lions are magnificent animals. They're a symbol of power, courage, and mobility often used on family crests, coats of arms, and national flags. Lions have developed a social system based on teamwork and a division of labor within the pride. A lion's roar can be heard from five miles away!

Marvelous, Mirthful, Mischievous Meerkats are extremely social animals who live together in burrows they dig with their long, sharp claws. Each one in a "mob" helps to forage for food, look out for predators, and care for the young. Fathers and siblings teach the babies to play and forage. Young meerkats are so fearful of predatory birds that even airplanes will send them diving for cover!

Native, Noteworthy, Nurturing Nubian Ibex are active during the day, browsing and scaling canyon walls. If threatened, an ibex rises up on its strong hind legs and points those intimidating horns toward the predator. Leopards, eagles, and bearded vultures are its main predators. Nubian Ibex are known for their milk, which is used to make cheese and soap!

Outstanding, Observant, Optimistic Otters are semi-aquatic and usually nocturnal. They eat fish, crustaceans, amphibians, reptiles, birds, eggs, insects, and worms. Eurasian Otters are playful creatures. Their predators are birds of prey, crocodiles, and dogs.

Playful, Passionate, Perky Fairy Penguins are also called Little Penguins or Blue Penguins. They're only 13-17 inches tall! These little penguins can dive as deep as 180 feet, but usually dive less than ten feet. They feed on crustaceans, cephalopods, small clupeoid fish, arrow squid, red cod, anchovies, and baracuda.

Quick, Quaint, Quackish Common Quail are ground-nesting game birds in the pheasant family. Some clutches of eggs can reach 20 or more in number. Both males and females care for their chicks. There are 43 different species of quail!

Remarkable, Resolute, Reliable White Rhinoceros is Africa's armored giant! A White Rhino can weigh over three tons, which is amazing, given that they mainly eat grasses and leaves. A group of rhinos is called a crash. They communicate through honks, sneezes, and poo. They are the largest of the five rhino species.

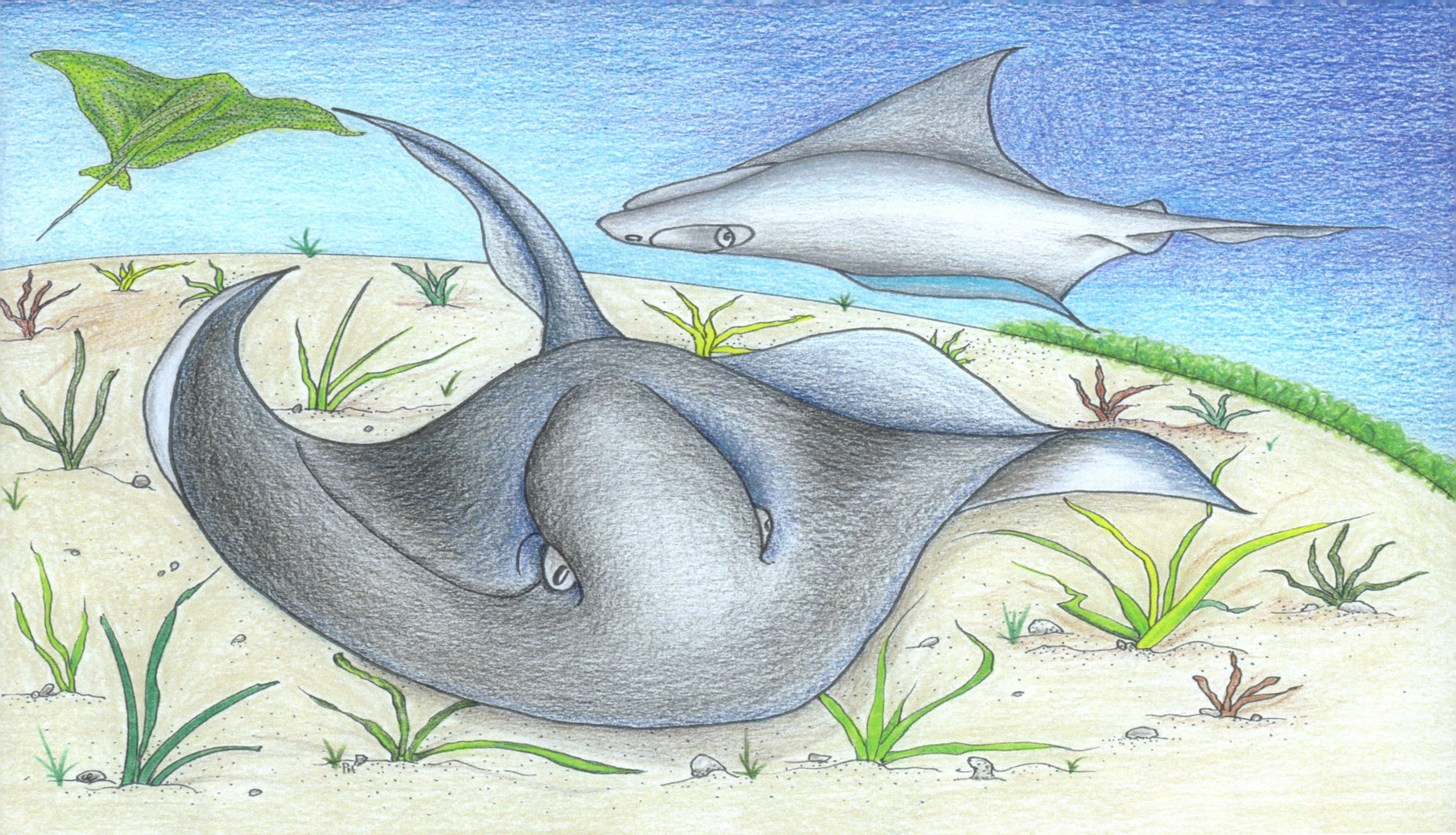

Sassy, Sagacious, Sly Cow-tail Stingray may be over nine feet long and five feet across! They are found on sandy bottoms in coastal waters and on coral reefs to a depth of 200 feet. They are preyed on by sharks, seals, sea lions, killer whales, and bottlenose dolphins. When a stingray feels threatened, it is likely to react by swinging its unusual tail upward, causing the barb to pierce the skin and inject venom.

Tenacious, Terse, Talented Tigerfish are the most aggressive fish in the world. These goliath tigerfish have a powerful bite force due to strong jaws, large teeth, and an interlocking beartrap-like bite. Surprisingly, they are very sensitive to air, light, and temperature. Tigerfish are found in freshwater rivers and lakes throughout Africa!

Underrated, Unique, Uncanny Sea Urchins use their tube feet to pick up small rocks, shells, and seaweed. They arrange these objects to cover their bodies as a form of camouflage. Sea urchins sometimes squeeze into a hole between rocks. If it's too small, sea urchins will use their teeth and spines to make it bigger for unwelcome visitors such as sea stars!

Vagarious, Valorous, Valiant Vulturine Guinea Fowl are also known as "Royal Guinea Fowl". When they hatch, they're almost fully developed and can fly within a few days. Their main predator is a hawk. They can escape from them by running at great avian speeds through the brush!

Whimsical, Wayward, Wandering Waterbuck's horns can grow to 40 inches long. Their body odor is so disgusting that it deters predators, including lions, leopards, hyenas, cheetahs, and wild dogs. Waterbucks inhabit areas close to water. Such habitats not only supply sustenance but also long grasses to hide from predators!

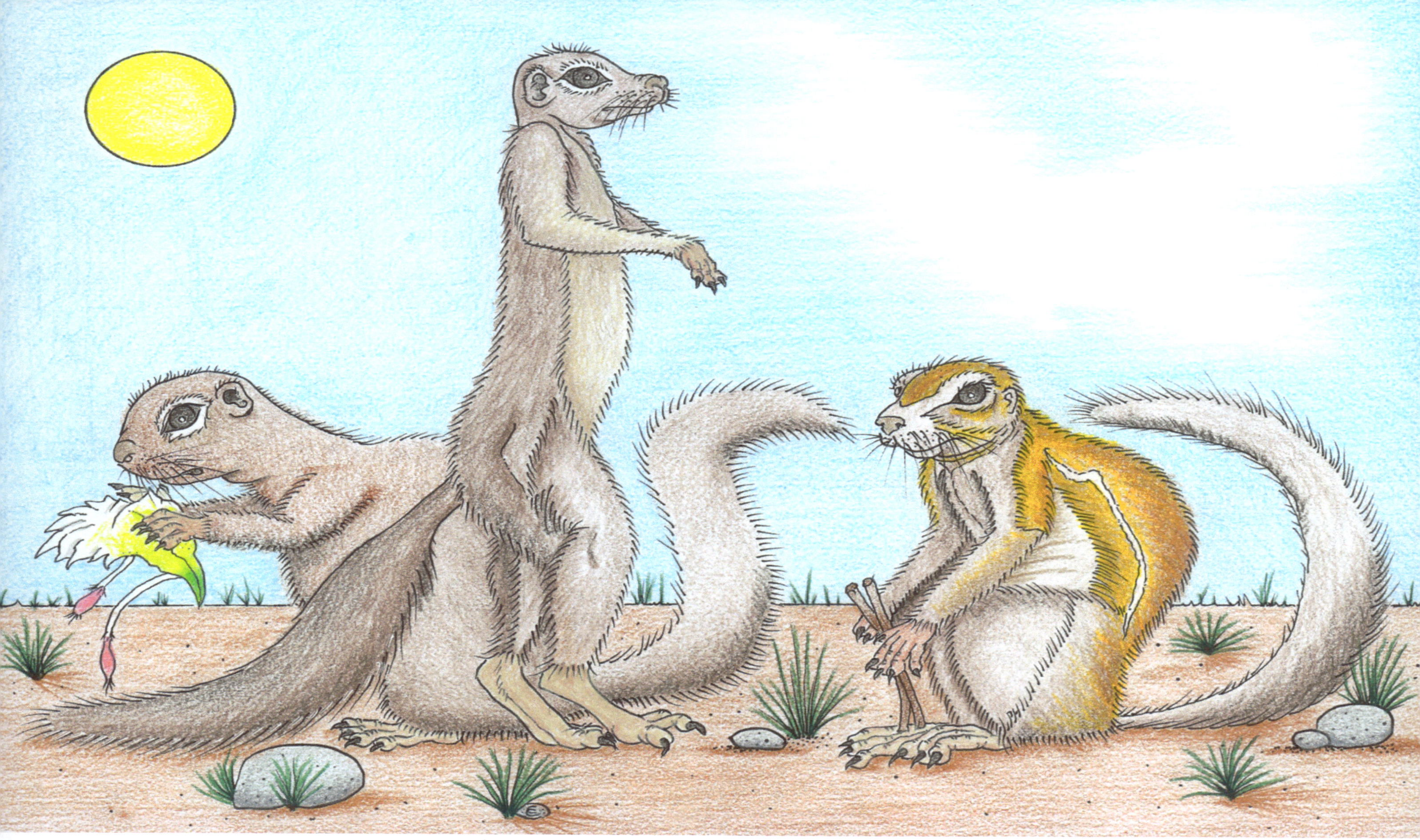

Xeric, Xenial, Xenodochial Xerus live in burrows. These ground squirrels inhabit savannas and rocky deserts in Africa. They use their fluffy tails as shade from the hot sun! Xerus hunt for food daily, and don't keep any in storage.

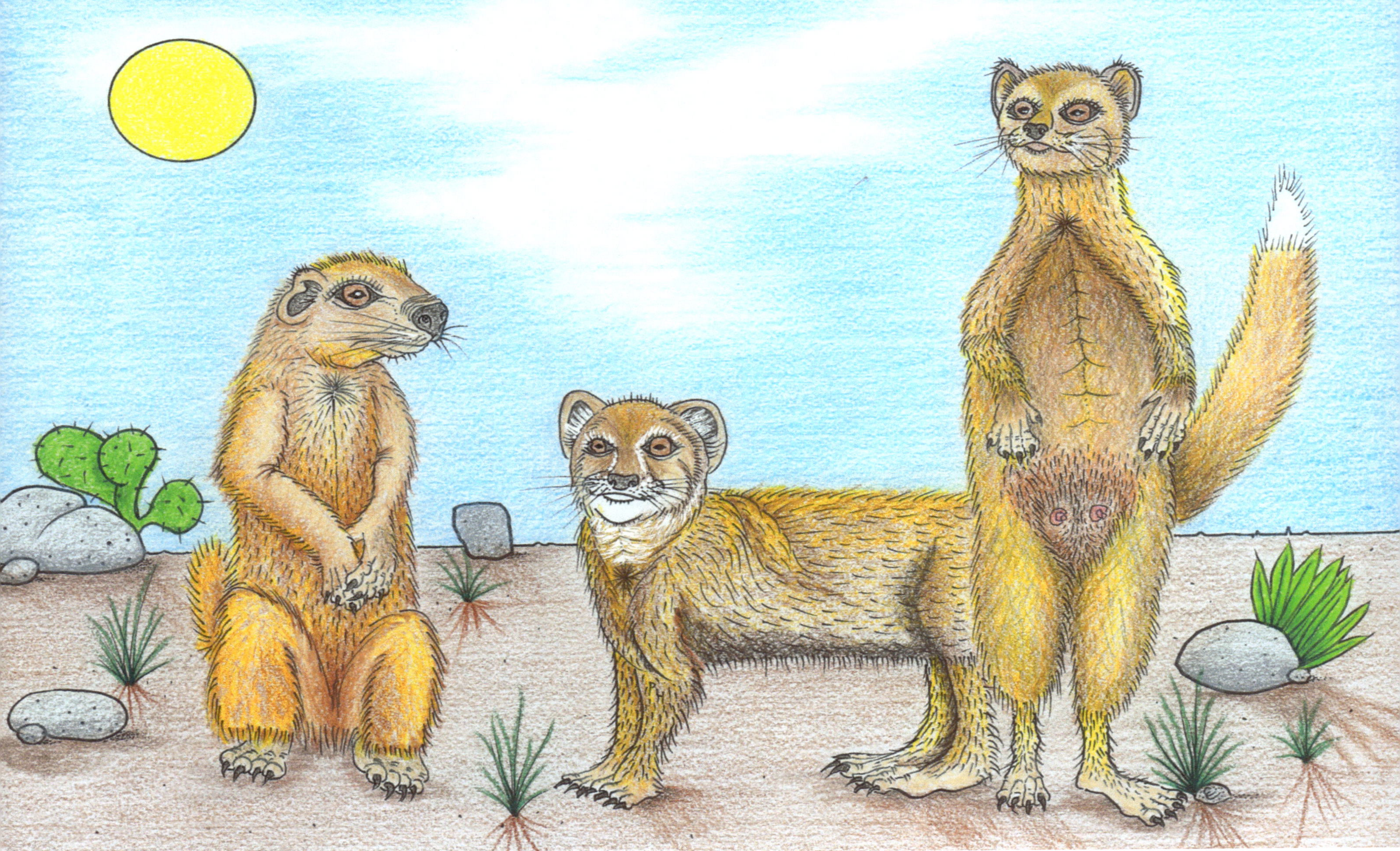

Yappy, Yare, Yearning Yellow Mongoose is also known as the Red Meercat. Their coloring varies from yellow to reddish brown. They are regarded as the most important rabies vectors on the central plateau of South Africa. Yellow Mongoose live in colonies of up to 20 in burrow complexes!

Zonated, Zippy, Zealous Zebra Eels are a species of Moray Eels. They can grow up to five feet long and do not have scales. To protect themselves against scrapes and parasites, they ooze a slimy mucus over their thick-skinned bodies. They are nocturnal and have no problem finding prey in the dark thanks to their excellent sense of smell!

Glossary
African Continent

Adorable: extremely charming or appealing

Astonishing: causing a feeling of great surprise or wonder

Attractive: arousing interest or pleasure, appealing

Beautiful: having qualities of beauty, aesthetic, pleasure

Beguiling: agreeable, charmingly attractive, or pleasing

Bodacious: remarkable, noteworthy

Charismatic: a special magnetic charm or appeal

Clever: mentally quick and resourceful

Courageous: mental strength to persevere and withstand danger, fear, or difficulty

Decisive: having the power or quality of deciding

Determined: having reached a decision, firmly resolved

Diving: to plunge or dash for some place

Eager: marked by enthusiastic or impatient desire or interest

Easygoing: relaxed and casual in style or manner

Elusive: tending to evade, grasp, or pursue

Flamboyant: strikingly elaborate or colorful display or behavior

Flirtatious: to show superficial or casual interest

Frolicking: to amuse oneself, make merry

Genial: freely expressing sympathy or friendliness

Grand: large and striking in size, scope, extent, or conception

Gregarious: marked by or indicating a liking for companionship

Happy-Go-Lucky: blithely unconcerned, carefree

Harmonious: having the parts agreeably related, congruous

Humongous: extremely large, huge

Impeccable: free from fault or blame, flawless

Imperturbable: marked by extreme calm, impassivity, and steadiness

Impressive: having the power to excite

Jesting: a ludicrous circumstance or incident

Jiggish: resembling or suitable for a jog or lively movement

Jubilant: feeling or expressing great joy

Kicky: providing a kick or thrill, exciting

Kinetic: active, lively, dynamic, energizing

Kittenish: coyly playful

Large-hearted: having a generous disposition

Laudable: worthy of praise, commendable

Lithely: characterized by easy flexibility and grace

Marvelous: causing wonder, astonishment

Mirthful: glee, cheerfulness, merriness

Mischievous: irresponsibly playful

Observant: paying strict attention, watchful, mindful

Optimistic: feeling or showing hope for the future

Outstanding: standing out, projecting

Passionate: capable of, affected by, or expressing intense feeling

Persistent: continuing without change in function or structure

Perky: briskly self-assured, animated

Quaint: old-fashioned or unfamiliar, marked by beauty or elegance

Quick: fast in development or occurrence

Quirky: characterized by peculiar or unexpected traits

Reliable: suitable or fit to be relied on, dependable

Remarkable: likely to be noticed, especially as being uncommon or extraordinary

Resolute: marked by firm determination, resolved, bold, steady

Sagacious: caused by or indicating acute discernment

Sassy: lively, bold, and full of spirit

Sly: displaying cleverness, ingenious

Talented: a characteristic feature, aptitude, or disposition of a person or animal

Tenacious: persistent in maintaining, adhering to, or seeking something valued

Terse: smoothly elegant, polished

Uncanny: being beyond what is normal or expected, supernatural powers

Underrated: rated or valued too low

Unique: being the only one, unequaled

Vagarious: impulsive, unpredictable, whimsical

Valiant: possessing or acting with bravery or boldness

Valorous: strength of mind or spirit, encounter danger with firmness

Wandering: not keeping a rational or sensible course

Wayward: opposite to what is desired or expected
Whimsical: lightly fanciful, unpredictable change
Xenial: hospitality or relations between host and guest
Xenochroid: having light-colored hair or complexion
Xeric: habitats with low moisture levels
Yappy: resembling or characteristic of a yap
Yare: characterized by speed and agility, nimble, lively
Yearning: a tender or urgent longing
Zealous: filled with or characterized by a pursuit of something
Zippy: very quick or speedy
Zonated: marked with zones or brands, belted, striped

About the Author

Debra grew up in a loving family in the Midwest. Her dad worked in sales, so they moved several times. She lived in Michigan, Minnesota, Iowa, South Dakota, and then again in Minnesota. She attended kindergarten in Decorah, Iowa, where she and her friend decided they would attend Luther College when they grew up. Her parents kept her and her siblings very busy to keep them out of trouble. They were involved with Scouts, a youth group at church, school activities, and 4-H. Much of their summer vacations were spent preparing projects for the Blue Earth County Fair. They performed a couple of their "Share the Fun" acts at the Minnesota State Fair.

During high school, Debra was a synchronized swimmer, a pom-pom girl, a dancer in Alouettes, a flute player in the school marching band, and a singer in the choir! While attending Luther College, she sang in the choir, was a member of the Tau Delta Gamma sorority, and studied very hard to become a teacher. School was never easy, and thankfully, her mother taught her how to use mnemonic devices to help her remember.

Her teaching career began at a private school in California. It was the perfect place to start with other new teachers from the Midwest. Debra also taught in North Dakota, Minnesota, and Arizona. In 2023, she retired after 42 years of helping kindergarten through fifth-grade students learn and discover the world around them. Debra earned her Master's Degree in Education from St. Mary's University while living in Minnesota.

She and her husband, Tim, met on a blind date at the Minnesota Orchestra's New Year's Eve event. Best New Year's ever! Debra became a "bonus mom" and now loves being grandma to their very special grandchildren. They enjoy traveling and spending time with family and friends living throughout the United States. At home in Arizona, both of them love being with friends, entertaining, reading, exploring, going to concerts, the theater, and sporting events. Now that they're both published authors, Debra and Tim look forward to relaxing and celebrating their writing adventures!

About the Illustrator

Patrick L. Hill is a mixed-media freelance artist based in Phoenix, Arizona. His skill set includes Cartoon, Whimsical, Realism, Commercial Illustration, and Graphic Design.

Early inspiration came from his father's natural artistic ability. Education came from Platt College of Graphic Design in La Jolla, California.

Experience comes from eleven years of employment at Mitchell International as an illustrative drafting technician and eight years of pool-site illustrative drafting for his own company, Fox Hills Pools.

Rooted in a passion for art, he continues to create illustrations for all ages to enjoy.

Watch for Other Books in Our Series

ASIA

NORTH AMERICA

SOUTH AMERICA

ANTARCTICA

EUROPE

AUSTRALIA

We Also Have Zoo Specific Books Soon To Be Released
We are seeking support to find the people who know people who are decision makers at your local zoo.
These books highlight the animals specific to each zoo, and would make an
excellent resource for sales in the gift shop and also for fundraisers. If you
know of such a person – please contact: timrilley@gmail.com

www.ingramcontent.com/pod-product-compliance
Lightning Source LLC
Chambersburg PA
CBHW042023050726

47602CB00009B/150